The Man In The Mirror:
Discussion and Application Guide

By

Patrick M. Morley

and

Joseph McRae Mellichamp

Thousand Fields Publishing
www.1000fieldspub.com

To men everywhere who desire to be
faithful followers of Jesus

The Man in the Mirror:
Discussion and Application Guide

THE MAN IN THE MIRROR: DISCUSSION AND APPLICATION GUIDE
Introduction

In his great classic, *Mere Christianity*, C. S. Lewis introduces a powerful illustration—Toy Soldiers or New Men?—to portray the choices God had in creating mankind. He could have created us as Toy Soldiers—each person perfectly made, all marching together in perfect formation, but Toy Soldiers nevertheless. He chose instead to create us with the potential of being New Men. His intention for us as New Men is expressed by the Apostle Paul in Romans 8:29: "to become like His Son."

How can this happen? How do we become like Jesus? In the Twenty-first Century, we like quick fixes, don't we? We would like to instantly become like Jesus, perhaps falling asleep one night as our old self and waking the next morning as a New Man, like Jesus. Unfortunately, it doesn't work this way. As one motivational speaker puts it, "One of the greatest reasons people can't mobilize themselves is that they try to accomplish great things. Most worthwhile accomplishments are the result of many little things done in a single direction." [Nido Quebin]

God has chosen to involve us in the process of becoming like His Son, one step at a time over the course of our lives. We have to roll up our sleeves and cooperate with Him as He leads us through the challenges of life, conforming us to the image of Jesus. The Twenty-fifth Anniversary Edition of *The Man in the Mirror: Solving the Twenty-Four Problems Men Face* has been fully revised and updated to serve as a sure guide to help you address and master the life challenges you are facing right now and for the remainder of your time on earth.

But *The Man in the Mirror* is not a book you can simply read, lay aside, and expect to have all your problems neatly solved and put behind you. We have designed the discussion and application questions in this Guide, to enable you, either in a small group or on your own, to systematically identify and address the challenges you face as a man seeking to follow Jesus as a faithful disciple. If you will diligently work through this volume, in conjunction with the book, when you have finished, you will be well on your way to mastering the challenges you face, and you will be equipped for whatever life experiences God has in store for you as you continue in the future.

Enjoy the journey!

Patrick M. Morley
Joseph McRae Mellichamp

PART 1: SOLVING OUR IDENTITY PROBLEMS
1. The Rat Race

Like a rat in a maze, the path before us lies ... Simon and Garfunkel from "Patterns"

You were running a good race. Who cut in on you and kept you from obeying the truth? Galatians 5:7

Carol and Larry

Many families in the U.S. today are experiencing a peculiar tension.
- Larry clearly understood the trade-off. More money, less family. More family, less money.
- The strain of keeping their household afloat discouraged them. There were bills to pay, kids to pick up, deadlines to meet, quotas to beat, but not much time to enjoy anything.
- Words from a Simon and Garfunkel song strike a familiar ring for many people: "Like a rat in a maze, the path before me lies. And the pattern never alters, until the rat dies."

The Problem

Do you know anyone who has ever won the rat race? Why do we compete in an unwinnable race? Could it be that we are not really focused on the significant questions of life:
- What is the purpose of my life?
- Why do I exist?
- How do I find meaning?
- How do I satisfy my need to be significant?
- Who am I trying to please, anyway?

The Standard of Living Fallacy

In general, there are two components to our standard of living.

1

- Our *material standard of living* which has soared in the last fifty years.
- Our *spiritual standard of living* which has plummeted in the same time span.

The desire for instant gratification has taken the place of deferring to a time when we can pay cash for our wants. Men today are worn out. Many who have chased their dreams have lost their families.

The most lasting satisfaction in life is our relationships, so why are we trading them off for careers with companies that will drop us like hot potatoes if we miss our quota?

The Dominant Economic Theory in America

- The dominant economic theory in America for the past forty years or so has been consumerism.
- We are *programmed* to consume, because the theory holds that a progressively greater consumption of goods is beneficial.

The Influence of the Media

The media in America is controlled by secular humanists. Secular humanism is the view that man establishes his own moral values apart from the influence of anyone (including God), and he self-determines his destiny—he is the master of his own fate.

The problem with this life view is that it has no absolutes, everything is relative—it has no external reference point. Our relativistic culture means that we need to guard our minds, because so many kooky ideas are floating around.

Through the media and advertising, we are consciously and unconsciously lured to go for the Madison Avenue lifestyle. And our problem may be more with what our unconscious minds are exposed to than our conscious minds.

Perhaps the only way to overcome this dilemma is to re-evaluate our sources of entertainment and information. Wouldn't we all like for our models to be in the sacrifices and contributions of scientists, artists, thinkers, missionaries, statesmen, builders, and other heroes and saints?

The Beautiful, Wrinkle-Free Life

Today, a lack of contentment pervades the life of the American consumer.
- The desire for things appears to have become more important than having a meaningful life philosophy.
- The result of trying to achieve the beautiful, wrinkle-free life, and failing, produces an excruciating anxiety level. Two components of anxiety are:
  - Media generated standard of living anxiety.
  - Debt anxiety incurred to support a lifestyle.
- We have exchanged our traditional values for a murky sort of prosperity, financed by a remarkable increase in productivity and by a suffocating load of personal, corporate, and public debt.

The Rat Race Defined

- We can define the rat race as the pursuit of the beautiful, wrinkle-free life.
- In pursuit of the good life, many men leave a trail of broken relationships.

Application Questions

1. The opening story of Larry and Carol is compelling, isn't it? Regardless of our personal situation, we all at times feel as though we are on a treadmill—working hard and getting nowhere. With what specific elements of Larry's situation can you identify?

_____
_____

2. Reread the questions on page 1 beginning with, "What is the purpose of my life?" Do you see that having well-defined answers to these questions could have prevented much of Larry's distress? Have you addressed these important questions? How?

_____
_____
_____

3. Step back for a moment and evaluate where you are with respect to chasing some desired material standard of living at the expense of your spiritual standard of living? Describe where you are now. Are any adjustments needed here? What are some action points?

_____
_____
_____

4. How vulnerable are you to consumerism? How much "stuff" do you have and to what extent does "stuff" drive your purchasing decisions? How much television are you watching? Other media?

_____
_____
_____

5. Now that you are coming to grips with the importance of you defining who you are and what is important, what are some initial steps you can take to get off the treadmill and out of the rat race? [Realize that this will be the focus of the rest of the study.]

_____
_____
_____
_____

2. Leading an Unexamined Life

The life which is unexamined is not worth living. Plato

Let us examine our ways and test them, and let us return to the Lord. Lamentations 3:40

Dempsey and Makepeace

Dempsey and Makepeace was a classic 1980s British TV show. Dempsey was a street tough New York cop, while Makepeace was a very feminine, very British, very proper English police woman.

Dempsey's view of the world was succinct: "Life is hard and then you die." Like Dempsey, many of us often wonder, "Why is life so hard?" and "What happens when I die?"

The Problem

As we saw in the episode of Larry and Carol in the last chapter, life often can be difficult if we don't take time to reflect on the *why* questions of life.
- The number one problem of man at the beginning of the Twenty-first Century is that he leads an unexamined life.
- We rush from task to task, but we don't call enough time-outs to reflect on life's larger issues.

Not Everyone Thinks Like I Do

It only takes a few minutes in the employee lounge or at a social function to realize that people have a variety of opinions on almost every subject.
- Why do men think the things they think?
- Why do men say the things they say?

Everyone has a worldview. For most of us, our worldview results more from where we were born, who our parents were, and what schools we attended than from a careful examination of

5

issues. Yet, our worldview influences every thought we have, every word we speak, and every action we take.

Two Worldviews

There are two predominant life views in America today:
- The secularist believes that man is intrinsically good, he masters his own fate, self-determines the boundaries of his achievements and knowledge, and no moral standards constrain him apart from those he chooses at his own discretion.
- The Christian believes an all-powerful God created the heavens and the earth. This living, omniscient God possesses all knowledge, and He established absolute moral standards by which man is expected to abide. He is holy, loving and personal.

We have moved away from Judeo-Christian values toward a worldview that lets us self-select values based on whether they serve our self-interests.

The choice between a Christian worldview and a secular worldview is a choice between God's race and the rat race.

The Results of Living an Unexamined Life

John and Carol were a typical couple who found themselves shipwrecked when they struggled with worldview issues.
- John couldn't seem to satisfy Betty's appetite for possessions.
- Betty felt like John was copping out on his duty to provide.
They ultimately divorced and lost everything in the process. How could a Christian couple go so far astray?

Christians in Captivity

Today, Christians in America are a minority. Why is this? Because we lead unexamined lives, many good men—Christian men—have been taken captive and caved in to secular practices.

Allan Bloom in *The Closing of the American Mind* states that our society's openness is not one that pursues the truth with a dogged determination, but an openness which presses to be "open to all kinds of men, all kinds of lifestyles, all ideologies."

If we are going to live by the Christian worldview, we must pursue truth with a dogged determination and the first step in this process is to see ourselves as we really are.

The Two Yous

You must understand when you begin this process of introspection that there are actually two yous.
• The visible you is the you that is known by others.
• The real you is the you that is known by God.

We are who we are in our minds first, before we speak or act.

"Look at the Fish"

And how do you examine yourself? Look at the fish!

Conclusion

Have you been leading an unexamined life? The rest of the book will provide you with a framework to think about specific areas of your life.

Application Questions

1. What would you like as an epitaph to summarize your life? A good practice to develop is to collect sayings (verses, proverbs, etc.) which give direction in this regard. Do you have any?

_____

_____

_____

2. It is apparent that few Americans think deeply about their lives. What about you? Where are you in this regard? What can you do right now to begin thinking seriously about your life?

_____

_____

_____

3. If we were to examine your life, is there evidence that you are following a secular worldview? Any evidence you are following a Christian worldview?

_____

_____

_____

4. Are there really two yous? What are some things you could do today that would lessen the gap between the visible you and the real you?

_____

_____

_____

3. Biblical Christian or Cultural Christian?

A whole generation of Christians has come up believing that it is possible to accept Christ without forsaking the world. A.W. Tozer

Anyone who listens to the word but does not do what it says is like a man who looks at his face in the mirror and, after looking at himself, goes away and immediately forgets what he looks like. James 1:23-24

Marriages on the Rocks

I can't name ten men whose marriages are working the way they are supposed to. How can this be?

The Problem

Many men sense that something isn't quite right about their lives, but they can't put their finger on the answer. A century of consumerism and media influence has caused a shift in values: we live in a culture dominated by the secular worldview.

Two Impoverished Views

Francis Schaeffer in *How Shall We Then Live?* suggests that the majority of people today have adopted two impoverished values:
*   Personal peace. To want to be left alone, not to be troubled by the troubles of other people, to live one's life with minimal possibilities of being personally disturbed.
*   Affluence. An overwhelming and ever-increasing prosperity— a life made up of things, a success judged by an ever-higher level of material abundance.

A Third Impoverished Value

If religion is such a big part of our lives, why hasn't it made more of an impact on our society? Here's the problem: Although Christianity is apparently flourishing, many of us have gotten caught up in this increasingly bankrupt culture. And the unfortunate result is a third impoverished value—cultural Christianity.

- Cultural Christianity means to pursue the god we want instead of the God who is. It is the tendency to be shallow in our understanding of God.
- Cultural Christianity is Christianity made impotent. It is Christianity with little or no impact on the values and beliefs of our society.

Two Kinds of Christians

Jesus was the first to clarify the different types of people who would or would not associate with Him in the Parable of the Soils—Luke 8:1-15. The four soils in the parable represent:

- Group 1—The Non-Christian. Those who hear the word, but won't believe.
- Group 2—The Cultural Christian: Type C. Where "C" stands for counterfeit faith—their association with Christ is a matter of convenience, not conscience.
- Group 3—The Cultural Christian: Type D. Where "D" stands for defeated faith—their association with Christ is a matter of conscience, but they have been drawn into the secular mold.
- Group 4—The Biblical Christian. Those who trust Christ and Christ alone for salvation. They seek to live by understanding and applying Biblical principles.

An Ambiguity of Terms

As C.S. Lewis noted in his great book *Mere Christianity*, words can come to have ambiguous meanings. And the word "Christian" is such a word.

Thus, thinking in terms of *Biblical* Christian or *Cultural* Christian is a useful way to explain the wide differences in what professing people think, say, and do.

10

Lessons from Elementary School

The secular culture today is so polluted, that to be a cultural Christian means that your worldview and lifestyle are contaminated by these failed, impoverished values.

Frogs in Hot Water

Malcolm Muggeridge's frog in the pot illustration.

Too Busy

Many of us are busy doing things, but are not keeping our personal relationship with God in tune. We can become so busy that we live in defeat in important areas of our lives.

Market-Driven Versus Product-Driven

Cultural Christians often think that truth is relative—that it changes as circumstances change. The biblical Christian accepts Jesus' statement, "I am the way and the truth..." (John 14:6).

That May Not Be Such a Good Idea

The cultural Christian lives by his own ideas and the ideas of others. The biblical Christian lives by the Word of God and the counsel of the Holy Spirit.

Looking Out for Number One

Who is number one in your life? The answer may reveal whether you are a cultural or biblical Christian.

We must often make tough decisions. Do we interrupt our personal peace by putting Christ first? Do we cheerfully accept a setback in our standard of living? Or do we go ahead because "everybody does it?"

Obedience is the trademark of a biblical Christian. That is how we demonstrate our love to God and truth to a weary culture.

Self-Examination

If you think you are a cultural Christian, then examine the influences in your life. Is the church you attend a biblical church? Do your friends embrace the Christian worldview? To what forms of entertainment, media, art, and music do you expose your mind? Are the values you live by biblical or cultural values?

Patient for Change

We didn't get to be the men we are overnight, and we may need to allow some time, perhaps a long time, before we see our lives the way we want them to be.

A Look in the Mirror

The man in the mirror will never change until he is willing to see himself as he really is, and to commit to know God as He really is. Are you ready?

Application Questions

1. As we have seen, it is very easy to get sucked into the culture. Everyone around us seems to be pursuing personal peace and affluence and it is natural to just go with the flow. Are you doing anything to resist the pull of the culture? What specifically?

---

2. Many people today are cultural adherents of a religion. Many Jewish people are Jews by ethnicity; many Muslims were born in Muslim countries so they identify as Muslims; and many

Americans identify as Christians because it's American. Do you understand the concept of a cultural Christian? Explain it.

_____

_____

_____

3. In the Parable of the Soils, Jesus lays out the important distinction between non-believers, cultural "followers," and believers. Of the four groups presented in the text, which represent believers and which represent non-believers?

_____

_____

_____

4. Which of the four groups would you say represents your current situation? It is crucially important that you are honest with yourself here. If you cannot say with confidence that you are a biblical Christian, what do you need to do before proceeding ahead?

_____

_____

_____

5. Obedience to Christ's commands is a hallmark of a biblical Christian. C.S. Lewis in *Mere Christianity* writes that Christians need to daily reflect on the essentials of their faith. Are you? If not, what could you do in order to begin to get Christ's commands before you on a regular basis? If so, great; keep it up!

_____

_____

_____

4. Significance: The Search for Meaning and Purpose

The mass of men live lives of quiet desperation. Henry David Thoreau

I have come that they may have life, and have it to the full. Jesus, John 10:10

Howard Hughes

Howard Hughes' wealth and power were unmatched by any other man of his time, yet his final end is a stark reminder that money is a mortal god.

The Problem

What do you think is a man's greatest need? His need to be significant. The difference in men is how we go about satisfying our need to be significant.

A Man's Highest Hope

- If you were a really great man, what would be the most you might expect from history?
- A man's ultimate desire, if he is thinking clearly, is for immortality.
- How we decide to answer the two questions, "Who am I?" and "Why do I exist?" is a choice between two time lines: one that's eighty years long and one that lasts forever.

Inappropriate Ways of Finding Significance

Consider some common ways the world defines significance.
- Fame: A Few Short Memories. When we try to answer the question, "Who am I?" in terms of fame and worldly accomplishment, we select an identity that quickly fades.
- Possessions: Unsatisfied Eyes. We all use possessions to send signals that we are significant. The most fleeting significance comes from things.

- Power: What's His Name Again? Men who achieve significant positions of responsibility and authority in life run the great risk of identifying themselves exclusively with the position.

The Game of Tens

If you think a person can find lasting significance through the pursuit of fame, possessions, or power, play the game of tens.
- Name the ten wealthiest men in the world.
- Name the ten most admired men in America.
- Name the ten top corporate executives in America.
- Name the last ten Nobel Prize winners, any category.
- Name the last ten presidents of the United States.
  Or try another version.
- Name your ten best friends.
- Name ten family members who love you.
- Name the ten most memorable experiences of your life.
- Name ten people you think will attend your funeral.

The Self Gratification/Significance Distinction

- Significance is not possible unless what we do contributes to the welfare of others.
- If I make helping others my practice, a state of significance results.
- The difference between self-gratification and significance is found in the motive and attitude, not in the task.
- Accumulating wealth, power, influence, and prestige are self-gratifying, but will not satisfy a man's need to be significant in any lasting way.

Being a Doer

- "Do not merely listen to the word, and so deceive yourselves. Do what it says. Anyone who listens to the word but does not do what it says is like a man who looks at his face in a mirror

15

and, after looking at himself, goes away and immediately forgets what he looks like" (James 1:22-24).

- In your search for significance, have you sought a purpose for your life by studying the Scriptures? We must study Scripture to discover God's purpose for our life. Then we must faithfully be a doer of what God tells us.

Faithfulness

Today Europe is a post-Christian continent. Why? What would have happened in Europe if, in each generation after the Reformation, there had been a handful of faithful men who had Luther's courage to be doers of the word?

If you are not experiencing the full measure of significance you desire, answer the following questions.
- Am I trying to win the rat race?
- Am I pursuing significance or self-gratification?
- Am I disillusioned with materialism?
- Have I been looking for significance in inappropriate ways?
- Am I a talker or a doer?
- Am I searching Scripture regularly to discover God's purpose for my life?
- Am I a cultural or a biblical Christian?

Application Questions

1. Bob Buford in his book *Halftime* writes that men initially pursue success, but at some stage in their lives they turn from success to significance. In what ways have you pursued success? Significance?

_____

_____

_____

2. It is sobering to learn that the way we choose to pursue significance can make an eternal difference. What is your strategy for being significant? Need to change anything?

_____

_____

_____

3. Fame, possessions, and power are not bad things in themselves, only when we set them up as measures of our or someone else's significance? Are you OK in your pursuit of these things?

_____

_____

_____

4. Here is the Significance Test: "Does what I am about to do contribute to the welfare of others in a demonstration of faith, love, obedience, and service to Christ?" How can you incorporate this test in assigning priorities to various activities?

_____

_____

_____

5. Do you know God's purpose for your life? Can you think of anything more important? As William MacDonald writes in *Our Reason for Being*, "The great goal of your life is to glorify God and represent His interests on earth. Everything else is incidental." Will you commit now to regularly searching the Scriptures to discover God's purpose for your life? What definite steps will you take to accomplish this?

_____

_____

_____

_____

5. Purpose: Why Do I Exist?

Man's chief end is to glorify God, and to enjoy Him forever. Westminster Shorter Catechism

The Lord foils the plans of the nations; He thwarts the purposes of the peoples. But the plans of the Lord stand firm forever, the purposes of His heart through all generations. Psalm 33:10-11

Tom's Resume

Tom had reached the pinnacle of success, yet still ached for a sense of purpose in his life. Many men are like Tom.

The Problem

Achieving goals becomes an unrelated string of hollow victories, increasingly frustrating as more is achieved.

- The problem with goals is you have to keep setting new ones because achieving them doesn't provide lasting satisfaction.
- The fleeting satisfaction of a met goal begs the question, "Is there something bigger for my life than the routine of setting and meeting goals?"

Identity Versus Purpose

There are two aspects to finding significance:

- Identity answers the question, "Who am I?" We derive identity from understanding our relationship with God.
- Purpose answers the question, "Why do I exist?" The only purposes that will survive are the ones linked to God.

Goals Versus Purpose

What is the difference between a *goal* and a *purpose*?

- A goal is a specific objective we want to accomplish. We will know when we have accomplished it.

- Purposes answer life's larger questions—"Why do I exist?" and "What does God want me to accomplish?"
- Goals are *what* we do. Purpose is *why* we do what we do.

Eternal Purpose Versus Earthly Purpose

- God's *eternal purpose* for us is to seek His kingdom, by which we enjoy Him forever.
- God's *earthly purpose* for us is to seek His righteousness, by which we glorify Him.

Eternal Purpose

God's eternal purpose for us is to enjoy Him forever. This is the most important part of our relationship with Him. If He did not have as His purpose to give us eternal life (so that we can enjoy Him forever), then our faith would be futile.

Earthly Purpose

God's earthly purpose for us is to glorify Him by seeking His righteousness. There are a couple of dimensions of this:
- There is a sense in which all men are alike, God gives all men the same **universal** earthly purpose: what we are to be (character) and what we are to do (conduct).
- There is a sense in which each of us is unique; God gives each of us a specific call on our lives–**personal** earthly purpose. A **Life Purpose Statement** encompasses what we discover as God's personal earthly purpose for our life.
- Our Life Purpose Statement should be global in the sense of describing the overarching purpose of our life. It is profitable to develop similar statements for the various areas of our lives—relationship with God, family members, etc.

The Apostle Paul: A Life with Purpose

Paul is a great example of a life of purpose. Read it in Acts.

Application Questions

1. Who am I? Why do I exist? Identity and Purpose. Can you answer these two fundamental questions in a short sentence?

_____

_____

_____

2. Our eternal purpose is fundamentally about our relationship with God, which, for His children, is forever. Is this important? Crucially! Can you restate your eternal purpose briefly?

_____

_____

_____

3. Our earthly purpose is what God has called us to be and do over the remainder of our life on the planet. Are you behind or on schedule? What is your earthly purpose briefly?

_____

_____

_____

4. Do you have a verse or proverb which helps you articulate your life purpose? What is it?

_____

_____

_____

5. Now you are going to write a first draft of your life purpose statement. It is a draft—that means you can change it. So give it a shot.

6. The Secret of Job Contentment

The most outstanding characteristic of Eastern civilization is to know contentment whereas that of Western civilization is not to know contentment. Hu Shih

I have learned the secret of being content in any and every situation... Paul Philippians 4:12

Chariots of Fire

The movie *Chariots of Fire* shows the quest of two men to win gold medals in the 1924 Olympics. Their motivations were vastly different: one did everything for himself, the other for God's glory.

The Problem

Are you getting what you want out of your job? Is your job rewarding?
- According to published surveys, up to 80 percent of Americans occupy the wrong job for them.
- Men, made for work, must feel a sense of accomplishment and satisfaction in their work, or contentment will elude them.
- If a man is unhappy in his work, he will be unhappy everywhere.

Is Work a Curse on Man?

You might be surprised to know that work is not a curse that afflicts man because of the fall; it was the ground that was cursed, not work. Work is how God intended us to occupy much of our time in His plan for His Creation.

The Secret of Job Contentment

The secret of job contentment is not getting what we want, but redefining what we need. Three principles from Scripture should guide us in this effort.

Redefining Our Ambition

What is your career ambition? If you are like many men it is:
* To make a lot of money.
* To be significant, respected.

Pursuing these and other like desires is acceptable, but our motives must be (1) to please God, then (2) to please ourselves. This is the secret of contentment, not just in good times, but hard ones also.

If we are in the center of God's will for our lives, we can bear up under any amount of stress. But when we are out of God's will, even unbridled success can taste sour and bitter.

Redefining Our Boss

Who is your boss? Do you work for someone else or are you self-employed? To be content requires us to redefine our boss; it is the Lord we are serving.

Paul wrote in Colossians 3:22-23, "Whatever you do, work at it with all your heart, as working for the Lord, not for men, since you know that you will receive an inheritance from the Lord..."

Redefining Our Role

When we become a true follower of Christ, we must recognize that a change has taken place in our relationship with God—not just in our spiritual life, but in our work life as well.

God becomes our authority and we become stewards of His work and resources. This redefinition is illustrated in the story of a king going out to battle in Luke 14:31-33.

Daily Surrender

When we strive to control the future with our own plans, we choke off God's plans for our future. One day at a time. He wants us to redefine our ambition, our boss, and our role, and surrender to Him completely—one day at a time.

Application Questions

1. Os Guinness writes in *The Call: Finding and Fulfilling the Central Purpose of Your Life*, "A few people enjoy neither their work nor their personal lives; more enjoy their work but not their personal life; only a few say they enjoy both." Where are you on this spectrum? Do you enjoy your work? Your personal life? Both? What would you like to change?

_____

_____

_____

2. One of the first things we need to examine to ensure job contentment is our ambition. Only when we make pleasing God our primary concern at work will we be truly content. What do you need to change to make pleasing God your top job priority?

_____

_____

_____

3. Who is your boss? It really doesn't matter whether you work for someone else or you are self-employed, you need to function at work as though God is your boss. What would change about your work life if you truly worked for God as your boss?

_____

_____

_____

4. Have you come to the point in your relationship with Christ that you see Him as in control of your life and you see yourself as a steward whom He entrusts to manage some of His affairs for Him? If not, what would you need to change in order to do so?

_____

_____

_____

PART 2: SOLVING OUR RELATIONSHIP PROBLEMS
7. Broken Relationships

Happy families are all alike; every unhappy family is unhappy in its own way.
Tolstoy

Your wife will be like a fruitful vine within your house; your sons will be like olive shoots around your table. Thus is the man blessed who fears the Lord.
Psalm 128:3-4

How Do We Choose

I thought, "We've arrived!" My wife volunteered, "Yes, but at the wrong place." How do we know what we *ought* to do?
- Why not prioritize everything we do on the basis of who's going to be crying at our funeral?
- Why should we give ourselves to people who don't love us at the expense of those who do?

The Problem

No amount of success at work can compensate for failure at home.
- Many men are succeeding at work, but failing at life. In pursuit of the good life, most men leave a trail of broken relationships.
- "I was so busy taking care of company business that I never put my own financial house in order."
- "I was so busy trying to improve my family's standard of living that, before I knew it, my children were grown and gone, and I never got to know them. Now they are too busy for me."

Why Do Men Score So Low in Relationships?

God gave man the natural inclination to be task-oriented—referred to as the cultural mandate.
- The culture we live in values possessions and accomplishments higher than people and relationships.

- When is the last time you met a man who described himself in terms of the impact he is having on his children?
- Our culture has persuaded most men that significance is related more to our balance sheet and our title than to teaching our children and cherishing our wives.

Grumpy Men

How we are behind the closed doors of our own private castle is how we *really* are. That's the *real* you and the *real* me.
- "Other people don't create your spirit, they only reveal it." Our wives don't make us grumpy; we are grumpy people looking for a place to grump.
- The key to relationships is time. People know how much you value them by the amount and quality of time you are willing to spend with them.

Conclusion

No area of a man's life has more potential for improvement than his relationships.
- Do my wife and children know that I am for them by the way I spend my time?
- *If you don't have enough time for your family, you can be 100% certain that you are not following God's will for your life.*

Application Questions

1. Do you know the meaning of the term "table knocker?" When the professor knocks on the lectern or table, it means what is coming will be on the test! This is a table knocker: No amount of success at work can compensate for failure at home. Are you OK on this? Anything you need to change?

2. We all have more things on our plate than we can possibly do. How do you choose from among all the options? If you chose to prioritize based on who might cry at your funeral, how would that change your allocation of time and effort?

_____

_____

_____

3. "I was so busy taking care of company business that I never put my own financial house in order." Is this you? Do you have your financial house in order? Do you see the tie-in with relationships?

_____

_____

_____

4. What is most important to you? Your balance sheet and title or teaching your children and cherishing your wife? What evidence could you present to convince us that this is so?

_____

_____

_____

5. Do you spend quality, individual time with your wife and your children? How much? Is it enough to convince each of them that they are important to you? Do you need to adjust anything here?

_____

_____

_____

8. Children: How to Avoid Regrets

My child arrived just the other day; he came to the world in the usual way. But there were planes to catch and bills to pay; he learned to walk while I was away. Sandy and Harry Chapin

Fathers, do not exasperate your children; instead, bring them up in the training and instruction of the Lord. Ephesians 6:4

Swept Out to Sea

This chapter begins with the story of three men and one's 12-year old son who crashed a plane into the sea on an Alaskan fishing expedition. Two of the men were able to swim to land but the father and son didn't make it, because the father stayed with his son, rather than abandoning his son and saving himself.

If we are willing to go so far as to die for our children, why is it that we often don't seem willing to live for them?

The Problem

Survey results indicate that the average middle-class father believes he spends fifteen to twenty minutes a day with his kids.
*   The actual average amount of time each dad spent with his kids was thirty-seven seconds, an average of 2.7 daily encounters of ten to fifteen seconds!
*   The average American child watches in excess of four hours of TV each day.
    What practical steps can we take so that we really get to know our kids?

Freedom to Be Kids

Pat shares an amusing incident which illustrates how we can be more interested in stuff than in our children.
*   He was always uptight about the new scratches that showed up daily on their coffee table.

27

- His wife responded, "Leave my children alone! I'll not have you ruining a million-dollar child over a $300 dollar table."

We dads need to give them the freedom to be kids. Our approach should be to help them get through growing up.

Protection from the World

When we allow our children to be indiscriminately exposed to the secular culture, we risk losing their fragile, impressionable minds to secular values. The task is complicated by the Internet and Social Media. Our goal is protection not insulation.

- Children, not wise but foolish, discriminate best between that which makes them feel good and that which makes them feel bad.
- The duty and role of fathers includes protecting children from evil as well as teaching them righteousness.

Value systems and belief systems are primarily influenced by parents, teachers, coaches, professors, pastors, peers, music, movies, and television. We need to ensure that our children are exposed to the right people and media.

- Teaching children what to look for in a friend, and placing them in environments where such young people can be found is a gigantic contribution to their beliefs and values.
- Too bad that many things which feel good at first deeply scar the lives of millions of our young people—drugs, alcohol, sex.

These days when we misjudge, we tend to underprotect, not overprotect.

Encourage, Don't Embitter

Mothers love and stroke their children. Angry fathers handle the discipline.

- Angry fathers are everywhere. I once heard an angry father yell at his elementary-aged son, "Why don't you act your age?"
- These are the words penned by Boswell's dad: "Gone fishing today with my son; a day wasted."

No Replacement for Time

If your children turn out well, all of your other problems will fit in a thimble.
- If we end up with regrets over the time we didn't give our children, it is a pain that never goes away.
- As Lee Iacocca pointed out, no one says on his deathbed, "I wish I had spent more time with my business."

Guardianship Through Prayer

"Believe in the Lord Jesus, and you will be saved—you and your household" (Acts 16:31). Who prays for your children?
- *We can make no greater contribution to the well-being of our kids than to intercede for them in daily prayer.*
- You may find some adaptation of this list of prayer topics for your children and grandchildren helpful:
  - A saving faith.
  - An independent faith.
  - A sense of purpose.
  - A call to excellence.
  - A growing faith.
  - To be strong and healthy.
  - A desire for integrity.
  - To acquire wisdom.

Application Questions

1. It is shocking that the average American father spends 37 seconds a day (2.7 encounters) interacting with his children, thinking all the while that he is much more engaged. How are you doing in this regard? Does your calendar show a different story?

_____

_____

_____

2. And it is more than shocking that kids are spending in excess of four hours a day watching TV. What are they watching? Are you monitoring their viewing? Should you be?

_____

_____

_____

3. What about Internet and cell phone use? Are you monitoring your children's use of these activities? Do you know what your kids are seeing on the Internet or to whom they are talking on the phone?

_____

_____

4. Do you know who your children's friends are? Do you know their parents? Do you supervise their activities?

_____

_____

5. A woman wrote in to an advice column recently that she, her brothers, and her father were molested when they were growing up by her father's father. She related how devastated her father was for not protecting them. Are you protecting your kids?

_____

_____

_____

6. How much individual, face-to-face time are you spending with your children? Is this enough?

_____

_____

7. Are you praying regularly and specifically for your children? Not just, "Lord, bless my kids." But intentionally, using a list of prayer topics? If not, don't you think you should be? What topics will you commit to praying for them?

_____

_____

9. Wives: How to be Happily Married

Let the wife make the husband glad to come home, and let him make her sorry to see him leave. Martin Luther

Husbands, in the same way be considerate as you live with your wives, and treat them with respect as the weaker partner and as heirs with you of the gracious gift of life, so that nothing hinders your prayers. 1 Peter 3:7

Sound Familiar?

After thirty years, they have time on their hands, but they don't really have a relationship, nor do they know how to talk.

The Problem

Many couples live together more as roommates than partners. Their social and sexual needs are met, but intimacy as friends never develops.
- Most men are not unhappy with their marriages, but they don't really enjoy their wives—they are less than happily married.
- Men need to have a friend with whom they can let their hair down, someone they can really trust. Few men find that friend.

When marriages don't run by God's authority structure, regardless of whose fault, things don't work. Here's how God intended marriage to work.

The Role of a Wife

- One of a man's deepest needs is to be respected. "The wife must respect her husband" (Ephesians 6:33).
- Your wife's duty is to submit to you, which is the ultimate expression of respect.
- To yield to another person is impossible unless you respect them. You can be forced to obey, but not to respect another.
- The goal of this instruction is not to reduce women to servants, but to provide an authority structure in marriage.

31

- Where is your wife on the submit/resist continuum (Figure 9.1)? Have you promoted good relationships?

The Role of the Husband

- The Scriptural instruction to husbands is to love their wife (Ephesians 5:25-28).
- The kind of love Scripture directs us to is volitional rather than emotional. We are to love our wives volitionally, as an act of the will by choice.
- Where would you place yourself on the love/hate continuum (Figure 9.3)?

Four Types of Marriages

Four different types of marriage relationships are:
- Love and Submit.
- Hate and Submit.
- Love and Resist.
- Hate and Resist.

Most marriages which are still together but not working are Hate and Submit or Love and Resist because one partner has decided to hang in there and try to make things work.

- The Hate and Submit Marriage. This is the most common type of marriage that is not working.
- The Love and Resist Marriage. The feminist movement originally fueled the Love and Resist marriage syndrome.
- The Love and Submit Marriage. We have known only a handful of men whose marriages are really working.

Love Her as the Family Prophet, Priest, and King

How can you build a Love and Submit marriage? By functioning as prophet, priest, and king for your family (Ephesians 5:25).

- Prophet. A husband is to be the family prophet. He represents God to his wife and to their children.
- Priest. The husband is to represent his family to God, primarily through prayer. He is a mediator for his family.
- King. The husband provides for and offers protection for his family. He treats them with consideration and respect.

Time Together

Carve out time daily to be together, to cultivate a personal relationship.
- Harmony about family goals and problems comes from spending time resolving differences about them.
- A thirty-day experiment: spend twenty minutes each day talking with your wife.

Shared Responsibility

Our marriages will work better if we apply, by mutual agreement with our wives, the principle of 90-10, Both Ways.

How Do Marriages Get Into Trouble

Most marriages tend to break down because the partners are critical of each other.
- Power struggles over unyielded rights can doom a marriage.
- Our self-centeredness is oftentimes the root problem.
"When it dawned on me that my wife wanted to be a teammate and not a slave, I became angry—both at her for not capitulating, and at myself for being so foolish."

Sex!

No temptation causes more problems for men than sex. Our culture does not prize fidelity as one of its values. For a marriage to survive today, a man and his wife must be at least as committed to the institution of marriage as they are to each other as individuals.

Money

Financial pressure is the greatest pressure on couples today.

Communication

Only through dialog can we be certain that we are being understood.

Application Questions

1. It is not popular in today's secular culture, but the best thing you can do for your marriage is to understand God's plan for families and to follow it. Read Ephesians 5:22-6:4. How are you doing?

_____

_____

_____

2. Sit down with your wife and reread Ephesians 5:22-6:4. Is this new news? Discuss how each of you is doing on your God-given role. What are some things you need to change? Your wife?

_____

_____

_____

3. Can you think of examples of couples that illustrate the different types of marriage relationships: Love and Submit, Hate and Submit, Love and Resist, Hate and Resist? What are some admirable characteristics of couples you know in the Love and Submit category?

_____

_____

_____

4. Prophet, Priest, King. That has a good ring to it, wouldn't you agree? Give yourself a grade in each area—be honest, no one is going to check up on you. What do you need to do to get up to speed in each area?

_____

_____

_____

5. We probably all go into marriage with a 50-50 mentality, don't we? And we find that it is easy to be disappointed or to disappoint. Have you ever thought about a different approach—the 90-10 rule for both of you. Why don't you go first? What would it take for you to become a 90-10 husband?

_____

_____

_____

10. Friends: Risks and Rewards

Five years from today you will be pretty much the same as you are today except for two things: the books you read and the people you get close to. Charles Jones

Jonathan said to David, "Whatever you want me to do, I'll do for you." 1 Samuel 20:4

A True Friend

Robert's act of true friendship showed me how much God loved me, and I knew I would be all right.

The Problem

Do you have a close friend? Not just someone to call for lunch, but a genuinely close friend?
- At some point, men realize they need friends, but adult friendships are difficult to start and harder to keep.
- Most men have a friendship deficit. They don't know how to befriend someone or how to be a friend.
- We don't have anyone who is willing to just listen, to simply be a friend and listen, and not always to have a quick solution.

Friends Versus Acquaintances

There is a great difference between a genuine friend and an acquaintance.
- You'd be fortunate if you had three real friends.
- Are the men you consider friends really friends?

Friends Are Hard to Find

The Pop Quiz will help you assess your friendships. If you are unable to answer most of the ten questions with a "Yes," you probably need to consider developing some genuine friendships, rather than having acquaintances.

Too Close for Comfort

We sincerely want to have close friends, yet we fear letting someone get too close.
- We worry that if someone really got to know us, they wouldn't like us.
- We need approval, to be accepted by another person, but we fear the opposite—that we will be rejected.

Betrayed!

Everyone has probably had a confidence betrayed before. And when that happens it is difficult to repair the trust level.
- Few types of emotional pain sear as painfully and as deeply as that of betrayal by a friend.
- Trust, transparency, and vulnerability are the stuff of which true friendships are constructed.

Taking the Risk

If you want a real friend, you will probably need to be the one who takes the initiative.
- The price of friendship is personal vulnerability.
- Transparency must characterize a friendship.

Attributes of a Friend

- A friend is there when you need him.
- A friend keeps us on track—reality checks.
- A friend helps us crystallize our thoughts.
- A friend will listen, not offer a solution.

Application Questions

1. "You'd be fortunate if you had three real friends." That is a sobering assessment, isn't it? Think over your male acquaintances.

How many of them are truly friends, someone you could count on if the chips were down. Do you have more than three?

_____

_____

_____

2. Here is another sobering statement, "Most men don't know how to be a friend." Does that apply to you? What would you say is the most important element in a friendship? Are you cultivating friendships?

_____

_____

_____

3. How did you do on the Pop Quiz in the section "Friends Are Hard to Find?" Were you surprised? Anything you need to do as a result?

_____

_____

_____

4. "The price of friendship is personal vulnerability." Does that surprise you? How would you explain it?

_____

_____

_____

5. Consider the attributes of a friend on the preceding page. Are they true of the friends you identified in question 1? Are they true of you for the people who consider you their friend?

_____

_____

_____

PART 3: SOLVING OUR MONEY PROBLEMS
11. Money: A Biblical Point of View

The problem with money is that it makes you do things you don't want to do. *Wall Street*, the movie

A faithful man will be richly blessed ... Proverbs 28:20

We Need a Pool!

Todd's lifestyle put a strain on his family and weighed heavily on his mind. His wife Janelle supported him emotionally, but she too felt helpless.

One day Todd noticed that his neighbors all had swimming pools. He wondered if he could afford one. "How are people supposed to make financial decisions?" he asked himself.

The Problem

Sixty percent of men in an informal poll reported having financial problems. One man said, "I don't have any problems money can't solve."
- How would you rate your biblical I.Q. on money? Because the Bible says so much about money and possessions, it is easy to be confused.
- By winking at the Scriptures we don't like and cherry picking the ones we do, we create our own little theology about God and money.

One cannot serve both God and money; you are either a slave to God or to money.

The Power of Money

Money is not just a temptation for a moment of carnal pleasure; it is the temptation for us to be conquered by an inert, mindless master, one incapable of saving us from sin or satisfying the deep hunger of our soul for true peace, meaning, and purpose.

The Test of a Man's True Character

No test of a man's true character is more conclusive than how he spends his time and money.
- If you really want to know what is important to you, get out your calendar and your checkbook.
- Let's look at how we spend our time and our money—then we will know what's really important to us.

Out of Control

In Chapter 1, we saw that many men are chasing a higher and higher standard of living—we called it the Rat Race. Sometimes it takes a financial setback to realize this is happening.
- It is counter-cultural but money and things are not the measure of prosperity the Bible commends.
- God has promised to meet all of our needs if we are faithful and obedient to Him.

Thus, if we are feeling out of control in this area, it is likely the result of serving money instead of God.

Is It Money or Me?

We all need money, lots of money, to meet our family needs. Money is not some ethereal felt need; money is a real need.
- What is money? Money is simply a commodity, a medium of exchange. Money, by itself, is uncomplicated.
- God knew how much we would struggle with it—that it would be His main competitor for our affections.

So why is there such varying opinion on how to handle money?

Three Perspectives of Prosperity

Scripture presents three views on prosperity:
- Poverty Theology. The disciple of poverty theology believes possessions are a curse and has rejected materialism in every

form. The person who thinks one must be poor to be humble is mistaken.

- Prosperity Theology. The disciple of prosperity theology believes that you have not because you ask not. The theory is that one can create a binding transaction on God in which He is obligated to bless you. Many adherents to this approach live consumptive lifestyles.
- Stewardship Theology. The disciple of stewardship theology believes that God owns and controls everything. Possessions are a privilege not a right. Being a steward is more of an attitude, a way of looking at life as a caretaker.

Poverty theology exaggerates the role of sacrificial work, while prosperity theology overemphasizes the pursuit of financial rewards. The steward leads a balanced life, enjoying God's abundance while serving others in love.

Application Questions

1. Read Matthew 6:31-33. Is this promise true, or is it just smarmy blather? How does the verse apply to your finances?

_____
_____
_____

2. Do you believe that we can tell what is important to you by looking at your checkbook and your calendar—by how you spend your money and time? If we looked, what would we conclude?

_____
_____
_____

3. How do you feel about the financial area of your life? Is everything under control? Or, do you suspect things might be out of whack? Are you serving God or money? What would you need to do to begin to serve God in the financial area of your life?

41

_____

_____

_____

4. Do you know anyone who subscribes to poverty theology? Why is this wrong? What about the so-called prosperity gospel—anyone you know following this approach? See the pitfalls here?

_____

_____

_____

5. Carefully study Figure 11.2, which contrasts the three different money management approaches. Do you see the wisdom behind the stewardship approach? God owns everything. He promises to meet all of our needs, if we simply put Him first in our lives and follow His ways. He wants us to sign on as stewards of His estate. Will you become a steward now? What do you need to change to do so?

_____

_____

_____

6. How do you anticipate your checkbook and calendar might change once you have been serving as a steward for some time?

_____

_____

_____

12. The Four Pillars of Financial Strength

Entrepreneur's credo: A dollar borrowed is a dollar earned, a dollar refinanced is a dollar saved, and a dollar paid back is gone forever! Ted Miller

He who gathers money little by little makes it grow. Proverbs 13:11

Four Principles

Here are four principles of financial management that will revolutionize your life and enable you to become a faithful steward of the resources God entrusts to you.

Earning: Little by Little

The principle of earning little by little is certainly counter to today's culture. In the fast lane, the quick money is the way to go.
- But as the verse from Proverbs above tells us having a steady income is the best approach.
- Many men today are looking for "get rich quick" schemes, but these rarely materialize.

Saving: Little by Little, Too

The Nest Egg Principle reflects the qualities of the biblical view of life: quietness, diligence, industry, prudence, patience— little by little. Here is an illustration:
- Accumulation Plan:
  - Desired annual income at retirement. $40,000
  - Required savings each year (10 percent).   4,000
  - Average annual interest rate.   6.2%
  - Number of years.   40
- Results at Retirement:
  - Capital accumulated (Nest Egg). $651,000
  - Annual retirement income.   40,000

Because of the impact of compounding of interest, even a small amount invested over a long period will grow into a large sum.

Sharing: Where to Store Your Money

Scripture tells us to "store up for yourselves treasure in heaven" (Matthew 6:20). Here is how:
- Try a different perspective—putting a cap on your standard of living. Everything you earn beyond what you need to live and save for retirement, give to Christian work.
- Three Guidelines.
  - Give a proportion of every dollar earned in relation to how God has blessed you. A good starting point is ten percent.
  - Do your giving in secret to guard against any temptation to become proud.
  - Give your gifts as an offering to God, not to men. Don't seek the praise or approval of men.

The more we give to God's work, the more our hearts will be fixed on Him.

Debt: The Ability to Pretend

Why do men go into debt? Consumerism is the idea that progressively greater consumption of goods is beneficial; it depends on constant stimulation of our desire to buy things—anything and everything.
- There are two ways to acquire and accumulate: income and debt. Debt is easy, when income is not available.
- Men either earn interest or pay interest. Far better to earn interest on savings than to pay it on debt!
- Debt is a symptom; it's a symptom of a consumptive lifestyle. It lets us pretend to be someone we are not—for a while.

There are sound contemporary and biblical reasons to avoid debt.

Application Questions

1. "Surely you can do today that which seems impossible to do for a lifetime" (*Larkrise to Candleford*, PBS series). You can surely begin today to initiate each of these four principles, can't you? What do you want to do?

_____

_____

_____

2. There is much to be said for having a stable job with a steady income. It may not be flashy, but it is dependable. If you have such a job, be grateful; if you don't, what steps are you taking now?

_____

_____

_____

3. In *The Millionaire Next Door*, the authors write that one characteristic of high wealth individuals is that they are "fastidious investors." Possibly the easiest way to save is to participate in retirement programs. Are you fully participating in programs available at work? If not, will you start today? How?

_____

_____

_____

4. *The Millionaire Next Door* also suggests that many high wealth individuals live "well below" their means. See why this is important? It frees up funds to invest in God's work. Are you living below your means? Could you? How?

_____

_____

_____

5. Credit card companies call people who pay their bills in full each month "Free-Loaders," because they don't pay fees or interest. Wouldn't you like to become a Free-Loader? If you are in debt, how can you begin now to get out of debt?

_____

_____

_____

PART 4: SOLVING OUR TIME PROBLEMS
13. Decisions: How to Make the Right Choice

Once—many years ago—I thought I had made a wrong decision. Of course, it turned out that I had been right all along. But I was wrong to have thought I was wrong. John Foster Dulles

Elijah went before the people and said, "How long will you waiver between two opinions? If the Lord is God, follow Him; but if Baal is god, follow him." But the people said nothing. 1 Kings 18:21

Old Habits Die Hard

Even when we decide to change our way of approaching things, it is difficult. Why is this? Inertia.

The Problem

Decision-making determines *who* and *what* we are more than any other aspect of our lives.
- We all do exactly what we decide to do; we are the sum of our decisions.
- Virtually all of our problems can be traced to a poor decision— a decision made by a process that is barely understood.

Why is making good decisions so difficult?

The Priority/Moral Distinction

Aside from minor decisions, most other decisions tend to be either priority or moral decisions.
- Priority decisions are choices made between *right* and *right*. The only imperative in making priority decisions is to be wise—to choose between good, better, and best.
- Moral decisions are choices between *right* and *wrong*—there is the morally correct choice and the morally wrong choice. Correct moral decisions require integrity and God's enabling.

We will cover God's priorities in the following chapter and integrity in Chapter 21.

How to Not Make the Wrong Decision

Since effective decision-making seems so puzzling, and because the consequences of making the wrong decision can be devastating, knowing how not to make a wrong decision is critically important.

The best approach here is to follow the process Jesus used in deciding—this will keep us from making wrong decisions.

The Magnitude of Jesus' Decisions

Jesus was in the wilderness for forty days and nights during which time He was tempted by Satan. Because He always made the right decisions, we have One who was tempted as we are, but without sin. How did He do it?

How Jesus Decided

In resisting Satan's temptations, Jesus gives us three principles of effective decision-making.

- The first principle of effective decision-making: live by the Word of God. If a decision contradicts Scripture, it's a bad decision.
- The second principle of effective decision-making is not to put God to a test—don't put yourself in a position that requires a miracle to bail you out.
- The third principle of effective decision-making is always to worship God and serve Him only in your decisions. Avoid decisions that negatively impact worship and service.

Consequences

Every decision has spiritual and financial consequences.
- Since all of life is spiritual, it follows that all life's decisions have spiritual consequences.
- Scripture is very clear that following Christ will have financial consequences—some positive, some negative.

Forgiven But Still in Jail

One of the most pathetic moments in human history involved David's adulterous affair with Bathsheba and his murder of her husband. Although David confessed his sin and was forgiven, he still had to endure the terrible consequences.

Life in the Fast Lane

If you decide to get out of the fast lane, God will help you. He is not so much interested in your *position* as your *attitude*; in where you *are* as in where you are *going*.

Application Questions

1. "Virtually all of our problems can be traced to a poor decision." Every single one of us has made lousy decisions—no exceptions. We can either sit around with regrets, or we can determine to do something about how we make choices. Which will you do? How?

_____

_____

_____

2. The first principle of effective decision-making is to live by the Word of God. How do you intend to implement this principle in your daily life? What assistance will you need with this?

_____

_____

_____

3. The second principle of effective decision-making is to not put God to a test. How have you been guilty of this before? How can you implement this principle in your daily life?

_____

_____

_____

4. The third principle of effective decision-making is to make only decisions that positively impact your ability to worship and serve God. Might it be difficult to assess this up front for some decisions? Do you think you are up for the assessment task? How can you implement this principle in your daily life?

_____

_____

_____

14. Priorities: How to Decide What's Important

The constant desire to have still more things and a still better life and the struggle to obtain them imprints many Western faces with worry and even depression, though it is customary to conceal such feelings. Alexander Solzhenitsyn

"Teacher, which is the greatest commandment in the Law?" Jesus replied, "'Love the Lord your God with all your heart and with all your soul and with all your mind.' This is the first and greatest commandment." Matthew 22:36-38

The Grocery List

The object of setting priorities is to allocate limited amounts of time and money where God directs us. To do so without foresight and preparation would be like grocery shopping without a list. We spend our resources, but not always in the way we should.

The Problem

A priority is an activity to which we give precedence by assigning a degree of urgency or importance to it.
- Most men have not settled the issue of what their priorities should be.
- Among those who do know what they should be, too few live according to those priorities.
- Perhaps no other time of the week reveals more about us than how we spend Saturday morning.
- Saturday is like the discretionary income in our paycheck. How do you spend your Saturdays?

Does the way you spend this discretionary time reflect the priorities for which you would like to be remembered?

Establishing What Is Important

When we say "yes" to following Jesus, then we must adopt biblical priorities. They will be like a flashlight illuminating how we should spend our time and money.

Our Top Priority

If the Bible is clear on anything, it is clear on the subject of our top priority. Jesus Himself taught this, "Love the Lord your God with all your heart and with all your soul and with all your mind" (Matthew 22:36,37).

Implementation

The most practical way to demonstrate our love for God is through obedience which includes:
- Bible Study. Daily consideration of God's Word.
- Prayer. Bringing our needs before God regularly.
- Worship. Attending a Bible-based church regularly.
- Sharing. Giving your time and money to God's work.

The man in the mirror can do nothing better than look intently into the Word of God that gives freedom and discover the principles, precepts, and guidelines offered.

Priority Number Two

The Bible is equally clear on what is to be our second priority. "Love your neighbor as yourself" (Matthew 22:39).
- Our spouse, children, and parents should be highest on the list of "neighbors."
- And God thinks so highly of our relationship with our parents that He made it one of the Ten Commandments.

Rest

Another priority is rest. Our emphasis is always on doing, but God is interested in our rest.
- Jesus said, "Come unto Me, all you who are weary and burdened, and I will give you rest" (Matthew 11:28).
- The rest that Jesus offers isn't just for the physically tired, but for the emotionally and mentally tired, too.

The Fourth Commandment concerns rest (Isaiah 58:13-14).

Work

Work should also be a priority. The purpose of work is to glorify God with the abilities He has given us. This should motivate us to pursue excellence.

Good Works

A final priority is good works which includes:
- Introducing others to Christ. Evangelism
- Helping others grow and become like Christ. Discipleship
- Caring for the poor and needy. Charity

Different people can contribute in these three areas in different ways depending on their natural abilities and spiritual gifts (1 Peter 4:10-11, Romans 12:4-8, Ephesians 4:11-12, 1 Corinthians 12:1-2)

The Competition with God's Priorities

The world system competes directly with God's priorities. However, God knows that we face these choices; that's why He has shown us His agenda and what our priorities should be.

Application Questions

1. Do you ever get overwhelmed with activities vying for your time and money? Have you ever searched God's Word for His priority scheme for you? Have some verses?

_____

_____

_____

2. It is pretty clear that God Himself wants to be our first priority. What does this entail? Will you make Him Number One? How?

_____

_____

3. Our second priority is our neighbor, and that includes our spouse, children, parents, relatives, friends, and actual neighbors. How do you communicate to these people that they matter?

4. Rest is important in God's agenda, and the Sabbath is a way He has chosen to get us to rest. *In The Training of the Twelve* (1871), A.B. Bruce writes, "It was a holiday given by a merciful God to His subjects." What is your Sabbath practice? Need some changes?

5. In Ephesians 2:10, Paul writes, "We are His workmanship, created in Christ Jesus for good works ... that we should walk in them." What good works has Jesus called you to do?

6. Do you know what your spiritual gift(s) is(are)? If you've never done a spiritual gifts assessment, at www.gifted2serve you will find a 125 question assessment that takes about 10 minutes to complete. You will then get a report listing your most likely giftedness. Will you take 10 now?

15. Time Management: Doing God's Will

One of the greatest reasons people can't mobilize themselves is that they try to accomplish great things. Most worthwhile achievements are the result of many little things done in a single direction. Nido Quebin

There is a time for everything, and a season for every activity under heaven. Ecclesiastes 3:1

Time Management: Doing God's Will

Dr. Bill Bright, founder and for over forty years president of Campus Crusade for Christ [Cru], often said, "I try to prioritize everything I do in light of the Great Commission" (Matthew 28:18-20). And his actions over his lifetime demonstrated this commitment.

The Problem

In informal surveys Pat has found that time management is one of the biggest problems most men have.
- The time management problem is less a tips and techniques problem than it is a strategic problem.
- The real issue is a clear understanding of God's **purpose** for our lives, living by biblical **priorities**, and making **plans** which reflect God's will for our lives.

In this chapter we will look at some strategic aspects of time management.

From Purpose ... to Time Management

Here is the progression we need to understand: Our purpose helps us prioritize. Our priorities form a foundation for making plans and setting goals.

God always provides enough time to accomplish God's plans.

Time in Perspective

Time is defined as "a non spatial continuum in which events occur in apparently *irreversible succession* from the past to the present to the future." The question is how do we get in step with the way God wants us to use our time?

Discerning God's Will

Many of us follow a circuitous route when trying to discover God's will:

- Step 1: I tell God what I am going to do. "To man belong the plans of the heart" (Proverbs 16:1).
- Step 2: God responds. "Many are the plans in a man's heart, but it is the Lord's purpose that prevails" (Proverbs 19:21).
- Step 3: I beg God to let me do it anyway. "All a man's ways seem innocent to him, but motives are weighed by the Lord" (Proverbs 16:2).
- Step 4: Finally, I humble myself and listen. "Commit to the Lord whatever you do and your plans will succeed" (Proverbs 16:3).
- Step 5: God tells me what He is going to do. "The Lord works out everything for His own ends" (Proverbs 16:4).

The Most Effective Time Management Strategy

The most effective time management strategy is to eliminate the first three steps we just described. Before we take any action, we should pray and seek the counsel of godly men.

Efficiency Versus Effectiveness

Many men have difficulty differentiating between efficiency and effectiveness.

- Efficiency is doing the job right.
- Effectiveness is doing the right job right.

When we live as though all of life is spiritual—which it is—we translate the will of God into every area of our lives where it belongs.

Hard Work

One of the biggest disappointments in the management of our time is the theory that hard work will lead to success. Ultimately, the blessing of God determines a man's lot in life.
- The best time management tip is not to be so serious about ourselves and the importance of our contribution to our success.
- Hard work is a virtue—it has dignity—when it is part of a balanced schedule.

Things That Last

Are you so consumed with supporting a lifestyle or other personal ambitions that when you die everything will be left behind?

- The cardinal time management question is this: are you doing anything with your time that has the potential to last forever?
- If we truly want to make a contribution to forever, we should devote some of our time and effort to reaching the lost.

Often we don't share our faith with others because we fear we will offend them and they will dislike us. The truth of the matter is that half of the people in the world aren't going to like you anyway, so they might as well not like you for the right reason.

The Road to Greatness

Don't you marvel at the accomplishments of some men? How do they get so much out of their time? The Apostle Paul was such a man. The book of Acts details much of his ministry.

Conclusion

Our purpose, our priorities, our plans and goals—these determine how we spend our time, and how we spend our time determines who we are.

Application Questions

1. Read the Great Commission in Matthew 28:18-20. Do you understand how this command of our Lord affects you? Can you see how ordering your life around this challenge could revolutionize your life? How would it change your decisions?

---

2. In *The Seven Habits of Highly Effective People*, Stephen Covey advises us to employ a two-way classification in which we consider both the importance and urgency of tasks. You may want to check this out by Googling importance vs. urgency.

---

3. Do you understand the difference between efficiency and effectiveness? To be effective in life, one must know what one should accomplish—that is, one's life purpose. How can you be more intentional about allocating your time around your life purpose?

---

4. An interesting and instructive exercise is to consider how Jesus allocated His time. Read John 6:38. Jesus always did important

things, and He did not respond at all to what we would call urgency (John 11:6). What does His example say to you?

_____

_____

_____

5. We will be most fulfilled investing our lives in eternal things. We certainly need to work hard for our employers, we need to take care of our bodies (exercise and recreation), and we need to reach out to others. How are you doing in these areas? Need to make any adjustments?

_____

_____

_____

PART 5: SOLVING OUR TEMPERAMENT PROBLEMS
16. Pride

I am the greatest. Not only do I knock 'em out, I pick the round! Muhammad Ali

God opposes the proud but gives grace to the humble. James 4:6

The Acid Test

Notice how men treat servers the next time you're out, then watch how they treat their colleagues.

The Problem

The sin of pride beguiles every Christian man. It requires no effort on our part to get, but all our strength to keep out.
- Men want and need to feel good about themselves—to have a good self image.
- Pride is a sin of comparison in which we compare our strengths to the other fellow's weaknesses.

Two Types of Pride

The key to a proper type of pride is to not compare ourselves to others.
- Pride Type 1. Rather than testing our self-worth by comparison to others, we are encouraged to self-examination.
- Pride Type 2. A feeling of superiority brought about by looking down on others.
We like to compare our strengths against the weaknesses of others because it makes us look good.

Two Types of Humility

In the same way that there are two types of pride, there are two types of humility.

- Humility Type 1. Not thinking more highly of yourself than you ought.
- Humility Type 2. Thinking too lowly of yourself. Self-deprecation.

Keeping the Right Balance

We each walk a pride/humility balance beam. The trick is to walk with a proper combination of pride and humility.
- We don't look down on others, but we have tested our actions, and take pride without comparing our self to others.
- We don't think more highly of ourselves than we ought to, but we soberly think well of ourselves.

Too Much of a Good Thing

All men tend to become satisfied and forget who God is and what He has done for us. Scripture teaches that praising God keeps us from forgetting His work in our lives.

No Permissive Parent or Tyrant

Another cause of Pride Type 2 is an absence of the fear of God—to hate evil and to be consumed with reverence for God.
- A just God is worthy of our reverential fear. If he were not just, He could be either a permissive parent or a tyrant.
- A man who does not fear God becomes so proud that he cannot detect his own sinfulness.

The Fragile Male Ego

Much of what we do is to preserve the image we have of ourselves—making ourselves feel important.

Our Greatest Strength is Our Greatest Weakness

God prefers a humble sinner to a proud religious man.

Symptoms of Pride

We are all guilty of pride and should ask God to make us aware of it in our lives. Here are some symptoms:

- One symptom of pride is a dead giveaway—constant critiquing of others.
- Another is blindness to the needs of others. Are you sensitive to their pain?
- Unwillingness to associate with people of lower position is yet another symptom.

We are all proud to some degree. Some are just more humble about it than others.

Application Questions

1. In his great book *The Call*, Os Guinness writes, "When Jesus calls, He calls us one by one. Comparisons are idle, speculations about others a waste of time, and envy as silly as it is evil." Are you prone to compare? What do you need to do about that?

_____

_____

_____

2. "I say to every man among you not to think more highly of himself than he ought to think; but to think so as to have sound judgment" (Romans 12:3). What is your opinion of yourself?

_____

_____

_____

3. It is certainly difficult to keep a proper balance between having a good opinion of ourselves and being prideful. What would be some useful checks you could employ in this regard?

_____

_____

_____

4. How do you treat servers? How do your friends treat them? How do you treat subordinates?

_____

_____

_____

5. Some of us justify constant fault-finding with others because we have the "gift of criticism." Do you have this gift? What do you need to do about it?

_____

_____

_____

6. Do you associate with people below you? At work? In the community? Any corrective action needed here?

_____

_____

_____

17. Fear

The only thing we have to fear is fear itself. Franklin Delano Roosevelt

Take courage! It is I. Don't be afraid. Jesus, Matthew 14:27

Franklin D. Roosevelt

F.D.R. was already a distinguished public servant when tragedy struck—he fell victim to a severe case of polio. During his convalescence a fear of fire tormented him—that he would be trapped in a burning building.

Eleven years after being stricken, he was sworn in as the thirty-second President. The country was in the depths of the Great Depression. Like his legs, the country was crippled in fear. Who better to symbolize the paralysis people felt?

The Problem

Every man struggles with the emotion of fear. Fears of all sorts muscle their way into our consciousness.
- What do you fear? Failure? Rejection by others? Sudden disaster? Other men?
- Courage is the state of mind that allows one to face hardship or disaster with confidence and resolution.
- Fear is the agitated state of mind that cripples us from looking any farther than the hardship itself.

Why Am I Afraid?

To be afraid is not to fully trust God. There are three reasons that we choose to be afraid rather than trust God:
- The Bible tells us to "fear not and trust God," but we have been deceived so often by so many, we have doubt.
- Men find trusting God difficult because our experience tells us there's no such thing as a free lunch.

- We know we are really guilty and find it hard to believe that God will forgive us and remove the guilt.

The Cycle of Fear

The episode of Peter walking to Jesus in the storm (Matthew 14:22-31) illustrates how fear operates and is overcome.
- Step 1. Reality. We see the wind.
- Step 2. Response. We respond in fear.
- Step 3. Result. We begin to sink.
- Step 4. Return. We return to our source—Jesus.
- Step 5. Rescue. Jesus acts to undergird us.

What Is Faith?

Faith is being sure of what we hope for and certain of what we don't see (Hebrews 11:1).

Godly Fear versus Secular Fear

The fear of God is often misunderstood. What is the difference between the fear of God and other fears with which we struggle?
- We fear men for a very practical reason. Men have the power to give us what we don't deserve, or to withhold from us what we do deserve.
- We should fear God for an equally practical reason. God has the power to give us what we do deserve, or to withhold from us what we don't deserve.

John Witherspoon said, "It is only the fear of God that can deliver us from the fear of man."

Was Jesus Ever Afraid?

Absolutely not. He was tempted to fear in the Garden, but He never succumbed.

Four Steps to Overcome Fear

When we are tempted to fear, we need to unbundle our emotions and eliminate fear. Here is how:

- Step 1. Restrict emotions to agony and anguish.
- Step 2. Exercise faith in the sovereignty of God.
- Step 3. Submit our circumstances and attitude to God.
- Step 4. Wait patiently for God to act.

Application Questions

1. Every man struggles with fears. What do you fear? Be brutally honest here and try to identify any fear of which you are aware.

_____

_____

_____

2. Take your fears one by one. Which of the three reasons in the paragraph, "Why I am Afraid?" for fearing rather than trusting God is applicable to each of your fears?

_____

_____

_____

3. E.V. Hill, a famous pastor in the Watts area of Los Angeles, taught that when God heard Peter's prayer to save him, He was thrilled because it was challenging compared to other prayers offered Him that day. What do you think? Are you in a real bind? Do you believe God can deliver you? Will you trust Him?

_____

_____

_____

4. How does one restrict his emotions to agony and anguish in the midst of a crisis? Do you think meditating on Scripture might be a

good way to do this? Do you have any verses at hand on which you might meditate in a crunch?

_____

_____

_____

5. Have you submitted your circumstances and attitude for each of the things you fear to God? If not, would you do so now? Is there anything you need to do now while you are patiently waiting for God to act on your behalf? What?

_____

_____

_____

18. Anger

"I lose my temper, but it's all over in a minute," said the student. "So is the hydrogen bomb," I replied. "But think of the damage it produces!" George Sweeting

My dear brothers, take note of this: Everyone should be quick to listen, slow to speak and slow to become angry, for man's anger does not bring about the righteous life that God desires. James 1:19-20

Boiling with Anger?

What makes you angry? Are you calm in traffic? Do you lose it with your kids? When you see someone mistreated?

The Problem

What immediately came to mind? A time when you were justifiably angry? Or was it impatience?
- Occasionally we become angry for a righteous cause, but most of the time it's because we are selfish and impatient.
- I have never lost my temper at the office—I would never want my colleagues to think I couldn't control myself.
- Rarely a week goes by in which the sparks of family life don't provide good tinder for a roaring fire of anger.

Anger destroys the quality of our personal lives, our marriages, and our health.

Three Angry Men

Here are three fictional men whose anger illustrates the kinds of anger that beset us.
- Freddie Flash has a short fuse. His anger is a frequency problem.
- Cary Control rarely becomes angry, but when he does, look out. His anger is an intensity problem.
- Gary Grudge never becomes overtly angry; he plots his revenge. His anger is a duration problem.

What Makes Us Angry That Shouldn't

Seven reasons for anger stir up our sinful nature and hamper our efforts to live by the Spirit:
- Violation of our assumed rights.
- Disappointment with our station in life.
- Blocked goals even by good causes.
- Irritation due to the flow of life.
- Feeling misunderstood by others.
- Unrealistic expectations of others.
- Pathological/Psychological issues.

Except for the last reason which usually requires medical treatment, these reasons have two characteristics in common: *selfishness* and *impatience*.

Is Anger Ever Justified?

When we observe a miscarriage of justice against another, a controlled, focused anger—righteous indignation—can work for a positive result. Betrayal with malice by a friend or a malicious rumor that threatens our reputation are also just causes for anger. But our focus needs to be on avoiding anger.

The Promise of the Undeserved Curse

Proverbs 26:2 is a promise we can claim whenever we have been wrongly maligned.

What Happens When We Become Angry?

Our anger oftentimes has consequences of varying degrees depending on the situation:
- Often there are unexpected outcomes—injuries, property damage, job terminations, etc., etc.
- Sometimes there is damage to our health. Doctors estimate that 60 to 70 percent of disease is stress-related.

When Is Anger a Sin?

Ephesians 4:26-27 contains good wisdom to guard against our anger turning into sin. Read it and practice it.

Responding to Anger

Here are some spiritual guidelines on how to respond to the temptation to sin in your anger:

- Keep control. "A fool gives vent to his anger, but a wise man keeps himself under control." Proverbs 29:11
- Overlook offenses. "A man's wisdom gives him patience; but it is to his glory to overlook an offense." Proverbs 19:11
- Avoid angry men. "Do not make friends with a hot-tempered man, do not associate with one easily angered, or you may learn his ways and get yourself ensnared." Proverbs 22:24-25
- Appease anger. "A gentle answer turns away wrath, but a harsh word stirs up anger." Proverbs 15:1

Conclusion

Are you an angry man? Have you been kidding yourself that you are a pretty nice guy because everyone at the office loves you? Remember, how you are in your private world is how you really are.

Application Questions

1. Is anger ever a problem for you? Is it a problem for anyone in your family, either as a source or as a target? If so, what do you need to do to address the issue?

_____

_____

_____

2. Can you identify with Freddie Flash, Cary Control, or Gary Grudge? Which type of anger do you think would be the most difficult to address? Why?

_____

_____

_____

3. Reread through the seven reasons for anger. Do any of them apply to you? Obviously the last reason requires professional assistance. Do you see that the others are what we might call persistent—that is, they are likely to always be with us? What can you do to address any that affect you?

_____

_____

_____

4. Do you think the Scripture-based principles in the section on Responding to Anger can help you? What can you do to keep these four principles in mind as you live your life in a fast-paced world?

_____

_____

_____

5. Who you are in your private world is who you really are. That is pretty sobering, isn't it? Seeking conformity between our private persona and our public persona would be a good goal to have. What can you do to lessen the gap?

_____

_____

_____

19. The Desire to Be Independent

I am the master of my fate; the captain of my soul. William Earnest Hensley

I know, O Lord, that a man's life is not his own; it is not for man to direct his steps. Jeremiah 10:23

Independent Children

Even as small children, we have an innate desire to be independent. That's why we watch our small children like hawks (and our big ones too).

The Problem

We are raised to be independent. Our parents taught us to be independent with our lives and to make our own place.
- Most men are taught to pull themselves up by their own bootstraps.
- Men want to control their own lives. We want the freedom to chart our own course.
- There is a distinct difference between taking responsibility for our lives and trying to live independently from God.

The Human Potential Movement

It's true. We can achieve many worldly successes by the power of our might and the strength of our hands. The problem is that God doesn't want us to trust in man, but in Him.

Trust in Man and Trust in God Contrasted

Jeremiah presents a vivid contrast between the man who trusts himself and the one who trusts God in Jeremiah 17:5-8.
- The independent man has turned away from God and is never able to satisfy his thirst for significance and purpose.

71

- The dependent man trusts in God and puts his confidence in Him for all of his needs and for his significance.

The difference between the man who trusts in God and the man who trusts in himself is not in the circumstances, but in his response.

The Illusion of Power

What is power—genuine power? The kind of power we generally think of—human power—is impotent. Genuine power is the exclusive province of God and those to whom He imparts it.

The Turning Point

When we seek our own independent way we try to remake God the way we want Him, rather than know Him as He really is.
- The turning point of our lives is when we stop seeking the God we want and start seeking the God who is.
- We don't know God as He is because we have never really gotten to know Him as He is.

The ultimate escape from the treachery of trying to lead an independent life is to start seeking God as He really is. When we know the God who is, He will help us decipher His mysteries and show us how to attain the pinnacle of trusting completely in Him.

Conclusion

Men want to control their lives—it's our training and our nature. If we can be in control, then we can be independent of everyone and do our own thing. But God wants us to trust and follow Him.

If you are prepared to follow Christ and seek the God who is, whether for the first time or as a deeper commitment, pray the suggested prayer in the book before continuing.

Application Questions

1. How would you rate or assess your desire to be independent? Are you truly independent? Does God have a place at all in your independence?

_____

_____

_____

2. Do you see the difference between the independent man—the one who has turned from God—and the dependent man—the one who has turned to God? Can you think of any good reason why one might truly want to be independent?

_____

_____

_____

3. When we honestly seek the God who is, He promises to lead us through life, to meet all of our needs, and to give eternal life with Him in Heaven. Do you believe this? How has this changed the way you live?

_____

_____

_____

4. Have you settled the issue of who is in control of your life once and for all? Will you endeavor, as much as you know how, to follow Jesus as a faithful and obedient disciple?

_____

_____

_____

20. Avoiding Suffering

God prepares great men for great tasks by great trials. J.K. Gressett

We sent Timothy … to strengthen and encourage you in your faith, so that no one would be unsettled by these trials. You know quite well that we were destined for them. 1 Thessalonians 3:2-3

A Blaze of Glory

How far would we go to avoid suffering? We would never seriously want to be taken out by a bolt of lightning, but sometimes even the notion of leaving earth by natural causes would seem a welcome relief from the suffering.

The Problem

Life is a struggle. It is natural to want to live a stress-free, pain-less life, with clear skies and smooth sailing.
- The desire of most men is to be happy, to avoid pain and suffering, and to escape the bleak life that so many men seem to lead.
- The Bible teaches that suffering is part of God's order. We shouldn't go looking for it, but neither should we be surprised when it finds us.
- The plain truth is that when life goes our way we don't carefully examine our ways. If nothing else, suffering does get our attention.

Seven Reasons Men Suffer

Here are seven reasons that explain why there is suffering in this life.
1. An innocent mistake. We all make them and suffer the consequences.
2. An error in judgment. Usually the result of not following obvious guidelines.

3. An integrity problem. Sometimes we get in trouble because of dishonesty.
4. The environment changes. Laws change, accidents happen, illness strikes.
5. Evil happens. People do bad things which often have negative consequences for others.
6. God disciplines. God often uses suffering to mold our character or to cause us to change some behavior.
7. God tests. God often uses suffering to get our attention and/or to test our character.

If you are getting the idea that suffering is not easily avoided, then you have the right idea.

Resisting Suffering

There are five ways we attempt to avoid suffering:
1. We plead. We challenge God's fairness.
2. We compare. We claim we deserve mercy.
3. We pout. We feel sorry for ourselves.
4. We shout. We become angry and blame God.
5. We doubt. We doubt the goodness of God and fear.

After the Resisting

The solution to our suffering is not in how to get it over with, but in learning how to enjoy the fellowship of sharing in Christ's suffering, to not falter in times of trouble, to be anxious for nothing, to endure patiently, and to walk in the power of the Spirit.

Sympathy for Our Suffering

When we suffer we can be sure that Jesus knows exactly what we are experiencing. He suffered even as we do so that He can be our example in suffering. Hebrews 4:15-16 tells us, "For we do not have a high priest who is unable to sympathize with our weaknesses, but we have one who has been tempted in every way, just as we are—yet without sin…"

The Privilege of Suffering

Until you have been up against the wall, totally backed into the corner, all your resources expended, no more ideas from your own ingenuity, no more wise counsel from friends, all favors owed have been called in; until you have been totally exhausted and without hope—not just for a moment—but for weeks and months or even years on end; not until then will trusting the Lord ever move entirely from abstract to personal.

The Restoration of God's People

Avoiding suffering is impossible. Our posture needs to be to look favorably on suffering (James 1:2-4). No matter how rough your life gets, remember God loves and cares for you very much.

We can try to resist or avoid suffering, but every man is marked for suffering; it is a part of life which can be sweet if we don't try to run and hide.

Ready to Die

The Christian is ready to die for Christ, but, that said, it is more important that we enter the pain of our suffering and live for Him.

Application Questions

1. What kind of present or previous suffering have you experienced? Was it financial? Relationships? Health?

---

2. Can you link any of the seven reasons for suffering to the different ways you have suffered? Is it helpful to do this? Do you see that suffering is not always our fault? It is a given in life.

_____

_____

_____

3. Look back over the list of ways we typically respond to suffering in the section on "Resisting Suffering." Are you reacting now to suffering in any of these ways? Should you be? How can you change?

_____

_____

_____

4. Are you able now to look favorably on suffering in the way described in James 1:2-4? Will you adopt this as your first response to suffering now and in the future?

_____

_____

_____

PART 6: SOLVING OUR INTEGRITY PROBLEMS
21. Integrity: What's the Price?

If you tell the truth, you don't have to remember anything. Mark Twain

A malicious man disguises himself with his lips, but in his heart he harbors deceit. Proverbs 26:24

Who Are You?

In Chapter 2 we talked about the two yous. The visible you is the "you" that is known by others. The real you is the "you" that is known by God.

The Problem

Dishonesty is so obvious that we often miss how wholly and completely it tints every aspect of life. Many men are trapped in the lie of maintaining a "Christian image" for honesty, when in reality they wink at integrity every day.
- When we are all alone, with no peer pressure to keep us on the straight and narrow path, that's when our real character is put to the test.
- This issue is so important because unless we hold onto absolute integrity in every situation, no matter how big or small, we grieve God.

The Common Thread

What common trait did biblical giants such as Gideon, Moses, Samson, and David possess?
- God knew that He could trust these men when they were all alone.
- Integrity more than any other characteristic, distinguished their lives.

Their honesty was the mark which attracted God's blessing on their lives.

The Lower End of the Scale

When we think about dishonesty we usually think of the really big stuff.

- If we limit our thinking to major matters, we will miss the point that to be trustworthy with much, we must first prove trustworthy with little.
- When we are honest, a surprised world will give a second thought to the possibility that Christ can make a difference in a man's life.

The Ease of Being Greatly Used

Most men are so mired down in the quicksand of dishonesty that an average, hard-working man looks very good to God.

Thou Shalt Not Steal

All of the Ten Commandments require obedience on our part. Disobedience is dishonesty. For those dedicated to Christ, we take a pledge to be like Him. So anytime we break one of the Ten Commandments it is an act of dishonesty.

The Little White Lie

The fragile thread of trust upon which relationships are built can be easily broken by a little white lie.

The Narrow Road

George Burns said, "The most important thing in acting is honesty. If you can fake that, you've got it made."

Moral relativism says that if no one sees you cheating (or lying or stealing), then it means you won't get caught. If you don't get caught, then it's all right, because unless you get caught, you haven't technically done anything wrong.

The Three Reasons a Deal Goes Bad

Here are three reasons business deals go bad.
- Error in Judgment. Everyone makes mistakes—when you make a mistake, honestly communicate to others involved.
- Change in the Environment. The vagaries of the business environment—competitive or regulatory—come into play.
- Integrity. Lying to prospects, concealing information, withholding pay increases, and other such practices.

These things are of chief importance to God who is looking for good men.

Once and for All

During the course of a day, we each have scores of opportunities to deceive.
- If we must decide each time we make a decision whether we will be honest or not, we consume a lot of energy and run the risk of making a sloppy decision and compromising our integrity.
- By settling the issue once and for all, and deciding to always choose the narrow road, to always have integrity, we liberate ourselves from the bondage of making hundreds of daily decisions.

God will know that He can trust us, in little and in much, and He will trust us with true riches.

Application Questions

1. What we do when we are alone, when no one is watching is a theme that keeps coming up. What about you? Are you the same when you are alone as when others are around? What do you need to do so that you are?

2. Most men are so mired down in the quicksand of dishonesty that an average, hard-working man looks very good to God. Do you believe this? What do you need to do to become that man?

_____

_____

_____

3. We have seen often the influence of moral relativism on our culture—"it's not wrong unless you get caught." Are you engaging in any business practices, or other behavior, that would be an embarrassment to God, yourself and others if you were caught? If so will you stop them immediately?

_____

_____

_____

4. Have you settled the issue of integrity once and for all in your life? If not, will you do so now? If you have, what are some results you have seen?

_____

_____

_____

22. Leading a Secret Thought Life

The secret thoughts of a man run over all things, holy, profane, clean, obscene, grave and light, without shame or blame. Thomas Hobbes

We take captive every thought to make it obedient to Christ. 2 Corinthians 10:5

Our Thoughts

Why can't we gain control over the secret thoughts of fantasy, envy, lust, jealousy, wild ambition, the desire for money and power, and the resentments that float in and out of our minds?

The Problem

Are you living a secret thought life that is significantly different from the you that is known by others?
- Would you be embarrassed if your friends and associates knew what went on inside your mind?
- Each of us has a secret thought life, an invisible life known only to us—it is not known to others.
- This secret life is usually very different from the visible you, yet, it is the real you, the you that is known by God.

The Battle for the Mind

Every day we battle for the control of our minds. A continual war between good and evil, right and wrong, rages for control of our thought life. The real battlefield for the Christian is the mind.

Mind X and Mind Y

Applying Douglas McGregor's Theory X/Theory Y categories to the mind leads to some helpful insights.
- Part of our mind is controlled by our sinful nature—we'll call this Mind X.

- Part of our mind we have surrendered control to God's Holy Spirit—we call it Mind Y.

The sins of our secret thought life incubate in our Mind X, but we can choose to live by the Spirit focusing on Mind Y.

The Fuzzy Line

What is the difference between a temptation and an actual sin in our thought life? To understand the difference is to know where it is safe and where it is not.

Temptation Is Not Sin

The thoughts that enter our minds are not sin. Many men beat themselves up mentally because they have tempting thoughts.

When Temptation Crosses the Line

What is the difference between a temptation and an actual sin in our thought life?
- When our normal observations become abnormal preoccupations, we have crossed the line.
- "We can't help it if birds fly over our heads. It is another thing if we invite them to build nests in our hats." Martin Luther
- "Temptation is sexual attraction to a beautiful woman. Sin is walking around the block for another look." A friend

Concealing Sin

When we do cross over the line, what should we do about it? No thought or word is a secret from God. We should confess the transgression to God and continue walking in the Spirit.

Visibility to Others

The high visibility of our speech and actions helps us keep them to a high standard. But the low visibility of our thought life is not subject to peer pressure except for our own self discipline and dependence on the Holy Spirit.

The result of low visibility? We lead a secret thought life, often unruly, which we would find embarrassing for others to know about.

Visibility to Me

While others may take note of our sins because of their visibility, we may be aware or unaware of our sins. These low awareness areas are where some of the real battles for our minds are waged.

The Visibility/Awareness Connection

Figure 22.1 shows the relationship between the visibility and our awareness of our sins.
- *High visibility sins* are usually sins of speech and actions.
- *Low visibility sins* are usually sins of our private thoughts.
Awareness of our sins usually causes us to attempt to adopt group mores in speech and action.

Combining visibility and awareness we have:
- High visibility/high awareness—blatant sins, peer pressure.
- High visibility/low awareness—often nonbelievers.
- Low visibility/high awareness—these we need to address.
- Low visibility/low awareness—our blind spots.
If we will make a commitment to become more aware of our thought life, if we will pause occasionally and ask, "Why?" when our thoughts don't seem to be our own, then we will have taken a giant stride toward conquering our thought life.

The Mind That Plays Tricks on Itself

Unless we develop a solid understanding of how our thoughts, motives, and ambitions are shaped, we will have impure secret thoughts, wrong motives, and selfish ambition.

Conquering the Secret Thought Life

"Search me, O God, and know my heart; test me and know my anxious thoughts. See if there is any offensive way in me, and lead me in the way everlasting." Psalm 139:23-24

Take Captive Every Thought

The solution is to bring every thought captive; and if we find we have sinned, confess the sin and ask Christ to again take control. This is the essence of living by the power of the Holy Spirit.

Application Questions

1. What if, like in the comic strips, people could see your secret thoughts? Would you be OK most of the time, or would you be embarrassed? Are you exposing your mind to anything that could be enflaming your thoughts?

_____

_____

_____

2. Do you understand the difference between temptation and sin in this area of your life? Do you have a good rule of thumb here?

_____

_____

_____

3. We really don't have much trouble with high visibility sins, do we? And for that matter, if we are not aware of a sin in our life, it is up to God to show us this. So that leaves us with the high awareness stuff. What can you do about these sins?

_____

_____

_____

4. Taking thoughts captive is a really useful concept. We should be continually filtering our thoughts through the filter of, "Would this thought be OK with Jesus?" If a thought fails the test, we jettison it. We certainly don't want to dwell on it. Will you, starting today, take every thought captive?

_____

_____

_____

5. 1 John 1:9 is a great verse in this regard, "If we confess our sins, He is faithful and righteous to forgive us our sins and to cleanse us from all unrighteousness." Write this verse down and use it over and over as much as you need it.

_____

_____

_____

23. Accountability: The Missing Link

Our society displays far too little correlation between its purported beliefs and its behavior. Anonymous

The kisses of an enemy may be profuse, but faithful are the wounds of a friend. Proverbs 27:6

Dear Pastor:

I've tried to take a look at my life, to examine my ways, but the plain truth is I don't know how. I really enjoy your sermons. They move my emotions and spirit, but on Monday morning at 9:00 am when the phones start ringing and the customers start complaining, I just can't make the transition. I really need help.

The Problem

- We see men falling short of their potential every day. Why? Christians don't fail because they want to fail.
- One of the greatest reasons men get into trouble is that they don't have to answer to anyone for their lives.
- Every day men fail morally, spiritually, relationally, and financially; but not because they don't want to succeed.
- They fail because they have blind spots and weak spots which they think they can handle on their own.

The Purpose and Definition of Accountability

The purpose of accountability is nothing less than to become more Christ-like in all our ways and more intimate with Him. Here is a definition of accountability: To be regularly answerable for each of the key areas of our lives to qualified people.

Four areas of this definition are *answerable, key areas, regularly* and *qualified people*.

- Answerable. The answers we give in an accountability relationship are primarily for the *goals* we set and the *standards* we should live by.
- Key areas of accountability: The Accountability Iceberg depicted in Figure 23.1 reveals why accountability is hard.
  - Relationship with God.
  - Relationship with wife.
  - Relationship with children.
  - Use of money and time.
  - Moral and ethical behavior.
  - Areas of personal struggle.
- Regularly. The interval between contacts with our accountability partner(s) should be frequent and systematic.
- An accountability partner.
  - Pick men who have skill and wisdom, men you respect, men with whom you feel compatible and whose judgment you trust.
  - Be sure to pick someone to cover every area: moral, spiritual, financial, and relational.

The Difference Between Counsel and Accountability

There is a significant difference between counsel and accountability.
- Seeking counsel adds value to our decisions, but seeking counsel alone does not go far enough.
- To be accountable is to give answers to the tough questions we are asked about our lives.

The Difference Between Accountability and Fellowship

There's also an important difference between accountability and fellowship.
- Fellowship doesn't probe with questions because it has never been asked to do so.
- Fellowship doesn't have permission to delve into the private areas of another's life.

Why Men Are Not Accountable

Here are some of the common reasons men don't have accountability in their lives:
- They're unwilling to see the value.
- It's tough for strong personalities.
- Personal success makes it hard.
- One must become vulnerable.
- Structure—it requires organization.

Getting Started

Pick someone with whom you think you would be compatible. Have them read this chapter, and explain your intent. If he seems interested, then get started.

Conclusion

Accountability is the missing link in most of our lives. It may be the thing that enables you to synchronize your behavior with your beliefs, and keeps you from spinning out of control.

Application Questions

1. Do you understand why accountability is so important for those who sincerely want to follow Jesus? Is it the missing link in your own life? Are you ready to get going?

_____
_____
_____

2. Look over the key areas of accountability in the section, "The Purpose and Definition of Accountability." What is your area of greatest need for accountability?

_____
_____

_____

_____

3. Who are one or more potential accountability partners for you? Would you begin now to pray that the Lord will move in their hearts to join with you in an accountable relationship?

_____

_____

_____

4. Reread the list of reasons men are not in accountability relationships. Do any of these apply to you? Are you willing to open up to become accountable with one or more partners?

_____

_____

_____

5. List below the next steps you will implement in order to get going on this important part of following Jesus.

_____

_____

_____

PART SEVEN: CONCLUSION
24. How Can A Man Change?

Few people think more than two or three times a year. I have made an international reputation by thinking once or twice a week. George Bernard Shaw

The knowledge of the secrets of the kingdom of heaven has been given to you, but not to them. Whoever has will be given more, and he will have an abundance. Jesus, Matthew 13:11-12

A Big Question

Life is a big question mark. God is a big answer. Whatever the question, He is the answer.

Perhaps you are at a point in your life for whatever reason that you want to change—you want to go deeper into the spiritual life.

The Problem

Why do men think the things they think, say the things they say, and do the things they do? Now we want to know how to change. Patient, trial-and-error effort, diligently grinding it out on a day-to-day basis—that's the pathway to change.

Famous Last Words

Consider the last words of some famous people in history [and the others in the book].
- "It's a bit embarrassing to have been concerned with the human problem all one's life and find at the end that one has no more to offer by way of advice than 'Try to be a little kinder.'" Aldous Huxley
- A lifelong agnostic, W.C. Fields was discovered reading a Bible on his deathbed. "I'm looking for a loophole," he explained.
- "I die before my time and my body shall be given back to the earth and devoured by worms. What an abysmal gulf between

my deep miseries and the eternal Kingdom of Christ."
Napoleon

The Case for Daily Effort

The Christian pilgrimage is a moment-by-moment, daily journey. Here are some givens.
- The Christian must recharge his spiritual batteries every day— this is a necessity.
- Usually our spiritual lives march forward or they slip backward.

Practical Daily Steps to Change

Here are some things you definitely, urgently will want to work in to your daily schedule!
- Daily Bible reading and study coupled with prayer are the first essential for helping a man to change.
- When tempted, reject the thought and give thanks for power to overcome temptation.
- When you become aware of a sin, confess it and thank God for forgiveness.
- We must be willing to live in moment-by-moment reliance on the enabling power of God's Holy Spirit.
- If Christ is truly pre-eminent in our lives, we will want to tell others about Him. Be on the lookout.

The Sin of Partial Surrender

The challenge is to become a certain kind of man—the kind we have described in these pages, a man committed to the Christian worldview, a biblical Christian.

Conclusion

Christ wants you to lead an authentic Christian life. But it will require daily effort on your part.

Application Questions

1. Are you ready to go deeper in the spiritual life? In this book, we've considered a number of problems men face and good strategies for overcoming them. Are you ready to begin?

---

2. The famous last words of people are often tragic—and moving. A good exercise is to look at the epitaphs of the kings of Israel and Judah in the books of Samuel, Kings and Chronicles. What would you like your last words or life summary to be?

---

3. Look again at the list of daily steps to change. By the way, this list is not multiple choice; it is "all of the above." Will you commit right now to begin working these disciplines into your life? What next steps can you take?

---

4. Congratulations for thoughtfully answering the questions in this Discussion and Application Guide. You are well on the way to becoming a faithful follower of Jesus.

Made in the USA
Columbia, SC
15 November 2022

71311119R00059